Published in the United States
By Young & Brilliant LLC

First Edition Published January 2022

Written by Desireé Emmanuel
Cover Illustration by Desireé Emmanuel

979-8-9920966-9-9

For wholesale or workshop inquiries please contact us at **info@youngandbrilliant.org**

This Brilliant Mind's Name is:

Life Skills You Can Bank On!

I am in charge of my own happiness.

I am a leader and inspire others.

I am kind to myself and others.

I will make today a great day.

I can do hard things.

I am always growing.

TABLE OF CONTENTS

The Creativity Builders

UNIT 1

Unit 1 - Vocabulary Words

Read each vocabulary word and its definition. As you read the story, circle each vocabulary word when you find it.

1. **Generative AI**:A computer program that uses your ideas to help create new things, like pictures, stories, or songs.
2. **Brainstorm**: Thinking of and sharing many ideas to solve a problem or create something new.
3. **Mural**: A large artwork painted or drawn directly on a wall for everyone to see.
4. **Teamwork**: When people work together, share ideas, and help each other to reach a goal.

The Creativity Builders

Aisha loved to draw—on scraps of paper, cardboard, and even leftover grocery bags. Her best friend, Leo, wrote exciting stories about all kinds of adventures, from flying dragons visiting the city to spaceships landing on Mars.

One afternoon, they visited the community center. Usually a fun place for kids, it now seemed dull.

"The walls look so empty," said Aisha.

"And the books are all old and falling apart," Leo added.

"This place needs something new—something exciting!" Aisha said.

"But how? We don't have supplies, and my crayons are almost gone," she sighed.

Leo thought for a moment. "Maybe we can find another way to bring our ideas to life."

At school, their teacher, Miss Vega, noticed them talking about their problem.

"I think you two would love learning about Generative AI," she said.

"What's that?" asked Aisha.

"It's a tool that helps you create things, like pictures or stories, on a computer," Miss Vega explained. "You tell it your ideas, and it works with you to bring them to life."

"That sounds awesome!" said Leo.

Miss Vega showed them a simple program on her laptop. Aisha typed: A sunny park with kids playing. The computer created a picture of a colorful park with kids smiling and paying together.

Leo typed: *A story about a boy who builds a treehouse*. The computer helped write a whole story in seconds!

"This could help us fix the community center!" Aisha said, excited.

Aisha and Leo shared their idea with their friends Sofia, Carlos, and Maya.

"What if we make new art and stories for the community center using Generative AI?" Aisha asked.

"That's a great idea!" Sofia said. "We can make murals for the walls."

"And storyboards for everyone to read," added Maya.

The friends brainstormed ideas for the community center:

- Sofia suggested a big picture of kids playing sports.
- Carlos thought of posters encouraging kids to follow their dreams.
- Maya wanted stories about kids visiting exciting places.

They used Generative AI to create their first batch of pictures and stories. Everyone worked together, sharing ideas and improving the designs.

When they put their creations up at the community center, kids and families came to see. At first, everyone loved the new look.

But soon, they had questions:

"Why don't the pictures show kids like us?" asked a boy with glasses.

"This story is cool, but what about one with a pet dog instead of a cat?" said another girl.

Aisha realized they hadn't included ideas from everyone in the community. "We need to listen to more voices," she said.

The group asked their neighbors, "What would YOU like to see in the art and stories?"

With fresh ideas, they created new pictures showing kids with different hairstyles, families having picnics, and even pets. They updated the stories to reflect the things kids loved—like science, sports, and exploring their neighborhood.

A week later, the community center looked vibrant and alive! Murals of happy kids and community stories filled the space.

"You've made this place special," said the community center director.

Miss Vega smiled. "What do you think you've learned from this project?"

"We learned that Generative AI helps, but it's our collective ideas that make it meaningful," said Aisha.

"And working together with everyone made it even better," added Leo.

Prompt Engineering Practice

Scenario

Aisha and Leo want to create diverse stories for the community center using Generative AI. They need to write clear prompts to get the best results. Let's help them!

Who should be in your story, and what makes them unique?

Bad Prompt: *"Tell me how to cook."*
Good Prompt: *"Give me a simple pasta recipe with only five ingredients."*

Be very clear and detailed.

What should the story teach or show about diversity?

Write the final prompt!

Write me a story about...

Work with an adult to test your prompt!

Eli's Storytelling Machine

UNIT 2

Unit 2 - Vocabulary Words

Read each vocabulary word and its definition. As you read the story, circle each vocabulary word when you find it.

1. **Prompt**: A set of instructions or words you give to Generative AI to guide it in creating something.
2. **Prompt Engineering:** The skill of writing clear and detailed prompts to get the best results from AI tools.
3. **Draft:** The first version of a story or idea, which you can change and improve later.
4. **Revise:** To make changes to a story, picture, or idea to make it better.
5. **Imagination:** The ability to think of creative and exciting ideas in your mind.

Eli's Storytelling Machine

Eli had a notebook full of ideas—wild adventures, funny characters, and exciting endings. But no matter how hard he tried, his stories were always unfinished.

"I have great ideas," Eli told his friend Mia one afternoon. "But I get stuck halfway through. Then I don't know what to do next."

"You just need to write faster," Mia suggested, shrugging.

"It's not that simple," Eli said with a sigh.

The next day at school, Ms. Rivera, their teacher, said, "Today, we're learning about something called Generative AI. It's a kind of computer tool that can help you build fun stories off your ideas."

Eli's ears perked up. "Can it help me fill in the gaps in my existing stories?"

"Yes!" Ms. Rivera replied. "It's like having a storytelling machine. You just need to give it the right instructions—called a prompt—and it will help you write."

"A prompt?" Mia asked.

"A prompt is like giving directions," Ms. Rivera explained. "The better your directions, the better your results."

Ms. Rivera showed the class how the storytelling machine worked. She typed into the computer: Write a story about a pirate searching for treasure.

In seconds, the machine wrote: Captain Finn sailed across stormy seas, following an old map. He dug into the sand, hoping to uncover the treasure, but instead, he found...

"That's amazing!" Mia said.

"Can I try?" Eli asked, excited.

Ms. Rivera handed him the laptop. "Go ahead! But remember, your prompt needs to be specific to get the best story."

Eli typed: **Write a story about a kid who saves the day.**

The machine quickly wrote: *Sam was an ordinary kid, but when his town lost power, he figured out how to fix the generator and save everyone.*

"That's cool," Eli said, "but I want more action."

He revised his prompt: **Write a story about a kid who saves the day during a tornado.**

The storytelling machine wrote: *The wind roared as Jake raced to save his dog from the barn. The tornado was getting closer, and Jake had to act fast...*

"Now that's what I'm talking about!" Eli said, grinning.

Eli kept experimenting with prompts. He realized that being specific helped a lot.

When he typed: **Write a story about an animal, the story was too simple.** But when he typed: **Write a story about a brave dog who finds its family in a blizzard, the machine created something amazing.**

By the end of the afternoon, Eli had several new stories:

- A dog that saves its family during a blizzard.
- A kid who finds a treasure chest in an abandoned castle.
- A robot that helps its inventor win a science fair.

At first, Eli thought the storytelling machine would do all the work. But he quickly learned something important.

"When I don't give enough details, the story feels plain," Eli told Ms. Rivera. "But when I'm clear about what I want, the stories are way better."

"That's called prompt engineering," Ms. Rivera explained.

"You're learning how to guide the machine to create exactly what you want. That's a skill!"

Eli nodded. "So it's like being the director of my story?"

"Exactly," Ms. Rivera said.

By the end of the week, Eli shared his favorite story with the class:

A brave dog named Max raced through a snowstorm to find help for his family. The wind howled, but Max followed his instincts, saving the day just in time.

"Wow!" Mia said. "That's amazing!"

"Thanks," Eli said. "The storytelling machine helped me, but my prompts made it special."

From then on, Eli felt confident about writing. With the storytelling machine—and his new prompt engineering skills—his imagination could go anywhere.

Prompt Engineering Practice

Scenario

Eli loves coming up with story ideas but struggles to finish them. His teacher introduces him to Generative AI, a tool that helps create stories using prompts. Now, Eli needs to learn how to write clear and detailed prompts. Let's help him!

What kind of story does Eli want to create? (Adventure, mystery, funny, etc.)

Bad Prompt: *"Draw me a picture."*
Good Prompt: *"Draw a sunny beach with a re umbrella and two seashells in the sand."*

Be very clear and detailed.

What details should the AI know to make the story match his idea? (Characters, setting, problem, etc.)

Write the final prompt!

Write me a story about...

Work with an adult to test your prompt!

Chloe's Garden Planner

UNIT 3

Unit 3 - Vocabulary Words

Read each vocabulary word and its definition. As you read the story, circle each vocabulary word when you find it.

1. **Layout:** A drawing or plan that shows where things will go, like plants in a garden or furniture in a room.
2. **Refine:** To make small changes to improve something and make it closer to what you want.
3. **Teamwork:** When people work together and help each other to reach a goal.

Chloe's Garden Planner

Chloe loved spending time in her grandmother's garden. It was filled with colorful flowers, buzzing bees, and vegetables growing in neat rows. Every time she visited, she helped water the plants and pick ripe tomatoes.

"I wish we had a garden like this in our neighborhood," she told her best friend, Raj, one Saturday morning.

Raj scratched his head thoughtfully. "That would be awesome, but where would we even put it?"

At school the next week, Chloe noticed an empty lot near the playground. It was a dusty patch of land surrounded by a chain-link fence. "What if we turn this into a garden?" she suggested to her teacher, Ms. Luna.

Ms. Luna smiled. "That's a fantastic idea, Chloe! But creating a garden takes a lot of planning. You'll need to figure out what plants to grow, how to arrange them, and how to take care of everything."

Chloe frowned. "That sounds like a lot to figure out. I don't even know where to begin!"

During their next science class, Ms. Luna introduced Chloe and her classmates to a new tool. "This is Generative AI. It can help you come up with ideas and plans for your garden. You give it instructions, and it gives you suggestions!"

Chloe raised her hand. "You mean it'll tell us exactly what to do?"

"Not exactly," Ms. Luna replied. "It's more like a helper. You'll still need to guide it and make decisions. Think of it as a tool to make planning easier."

Ms. Luna showed them how to type a prompt:
Plan a garden with flowers, vegetables, and a path for walking.
The AI generated a layout with rows of flowers on one side, vegetables on the other, and a winding path in the middle.

"Whoa!" Raj said, leaning closer. "It even shows how much space we need for each plant!"

The class worked together to refine the AI's suggestions. "Let's add a butterfly garden," Chloe suggested.

"And a bench where people can sit," Raj added.

With each new idea, they typed another prompt:
Add a butterfly garden with flowers that attract bees and butterflies. Include a small bench in the corner of the garden.

The AI updated the plan, and the design grew more detailed and exciting.

With their garden layout ready, the class divided into teams. Some students focused on finding the right plants, while others worked on tools and supplies.

Raj and Chloe took charge of deciding where each plant would go. "Tomatoes need a lot of sunlight," Chloe said. "Let's put them near the fence, where the sun shines the longest."

"But flowers like shade," Raj pointed out. "We can plant them under the tree."

They used the AI's suggestions as a guide but made adjustments based on what they learned from their research and Ms. Luna's advice.

The first weekend of planting was exciting but messy. Chloe accidentally spilled a bag of seeds, and Raj forgot to dig deep enough holes for the tomato plants. Some of the vegetables looked crowded together, and the flower seeds were scattered unevenly.

"This doesn't look like the plan," Chloe sighed.

"It's okay," Ms. Luna said. "Remember how the AI helped us refine our garden design? You can refine the way you plant too."

The class regrouped. They used stakes to mark rows and carefully replanted the vegetables. Raj made a chart to track which plants needed watering each day. Chloe added labels so everyone knew where the flowers, vegetables, and herbs were.

By the end of the weekend, the garden was neat and organized.

A month later, the garden was thriving. Butterflies fluttered around the flowers, and neighbors stopped by to admire the fresh vegetables growing along the path.

"This is amazing," Raj said as they harvested the first tomatoes. "We turned a dusty lot into something beautiful."

Chloe grinned. "And we couldn't have done it without teamwork—and a little help from Generative AI!"

Ms. Luna took a photo of the class standing proudly in front of the garden. "You see?" she said. "Technology is a powerful tool, but it's your creativity, hard work, and problem-solving that made this garden grow."

The garden became popular and very helpful for the community. The garden is a reminder that big changes start with small seeds of ideas—and a lot of teamwork.

Prompt Engineering Practice

Scenario

Chloe wants to turn an empty lot into a beautiful garden for her neighborhood. She learns that Generative AI can help plan the garden layout. To get the best results, she needs a clear and detailed prompt. Let's help her!

What should be in the garden? (Flowers, vegetables, trees, a pathway, etc.)

Bad Prompt: *"Make a birthday card."*
Good Prompt: *"Make a funny birthday card for an 8-year-old who loves dinosaurs."*

Be very clear and detailed.

Are there any special things to consider? (Small space, lots of sun, different seasons, etc.)

Write the final prompt!

Help me plan a garden layout for...

Work with an adult to test your prompt!

The Big Brainstorm

UNIT 4

Unit 4 - Vocabulary Words

Read each vocabulary word and its definition. As you read the story, circle each vocabulary word when you find it.

1. **ProStencil:** A cut-out shape used to trace or paint the same design.

The Big Brainstorm

Tia and Jay lived in a buzzing apartment complex where neighbors waved from balconies, children played tag in the courtyard, and music drifted through open windows. Their favorite event of the year was the neighborhood block party—a festival full of food, music, and laughter.

This year, as they helped hand out flyers with Miss Rosa, the festival organizer, they overheard her talking to their grandmother.

"We need more decorations," Miss Rosa said, shaking her head. "But we don't have the budget for anything fancy."

Tia frowned. "It sounds like Miss Rosa really wants the party to feel special," she whispered to Jay.

"Yeah, but how can we help?" Jay replied. "We don't have art supplies—or, let's face it, great art skills."

That night, they sat at the kitchen table, trying to think of ideas. Tia doodled circles on the back of an old receipt, and Jay stared at the blank paper in front of him.

"This feels impossible," Tia groaned. "How do we make decorations without supplies?"

"It's like trying to make a sandwich without bread," Jay added, leaning back in his chair.

Their grandmother, overhearing their conversation, smiled and joined them at the table. "What's got you two looking so defeated?"

Tia explained the problem while Jay held up his paper. "We want to help Miss Rosa, but we don't know where to start."

Grandma opened her laptop. "Have you heard of Generative AI?"

Jay squinted. "What's that? Some kind of robot?"

"Not exactly," Grandma said. "It's a computer program. You type in what you're imagining, and it gives you ideas—pictures, patterns, or even decorations. It's not magic, but it feels like it!"

Tia's eyes lit up. "Wait, so it can help us design decorations?"

"Exactly," Grandma said,pulling it up on her screen.

"Let's try it. What would you like to see?"

Jay leaned forward. "Let's start with something simple. How about... colorful flowers for the party?"

Grandma typed: **Colorful flower decorations for a block party.** In seconds, the screen filled with vibrant designs—some as banners, others as stencils, and a few that looked like paper cut-outs.

"Whoa!" Tia exclaimed. "This is amazing! It's like the computer knows what we're thinking!"

"Not exactly," Grandma said. "The AI learned from lots of examples, and it uses those patterns to make something new. But you still have to guide it—tell it what works and what doesn't."

"Okay," Jay said. "Let's keep experimenting!"

Excited, Tia grabbed a notebook and started writing down their ideas. "We need flowers, but we should also add banners and something fun for the tables."

Jay nodded. "How about balloons with cool patterns? And maybe stencils we can paint onto cardboard?"

They typed prompts into the AI one by one:

- **Design a banner with bright, colorful shapes.**
- **Create patterns for balloons with stars and hearts.**
- **Show table decorations with flowers and stripes.**

Each time, the AI generated unique designs. Some were simple, while others were over-the-top and silly. "This one looks like a flower monster," Jay said, laughing.

Tia pointed to one design. "This would make a great stencil! Miss Rosa could cut it out of old cardboard to save money."

By the time they finished, they had a full folder of creative ideas ready to share.

The next morning, Tia and Jay showed Miss Rosa the designs. She clapped her hands in delight. "These are perfect! Let's try a few."

Using old cardboard boxes from the grocery store, they cut out stencils and tested them with paint. At first, things didn't go smoothly. One stencil was too detailed to cut easily, and another design's dark colors didn't stand out.

"This isn't working," Tia said, frustrated.

Miss Rosa smiled. "Remember, it's okay to make mistakes. Think of this as a first draft. How can we make it better?"

Tia and Jay thought for a moment, then updated their prompts:

- **Make simple flower shapes with bold lines.**
- **Use bright, cheerful colors that stand out.**

The AI delivered improved designs, which they printed and tested again. This time, the stencils were easy to use, and the colors popped against the cardboard.

Jay grinned. "Now we're getting somewhere!"

On the day of the block party, the neighborhood was transformed. Bright paper flowers lined the fences, balloons with star patterns floated in the breeze, and colorful banners stretched across the streets.

"This looks incredible!" one neighbor said. Another added, "It's amazing what you can do without spending much money!"

Miss Rosa took the microphone to thank Tia and Jay. "These two used their creativity and some cool new tools to make this festival extra special. Let's give them a big round of applause!"

As the crowd cheered, Tia leaned over to Jay. "You know what the best part is?"

Jay nodded. "Making everyone happy?"

"Exactly," Tia said. "Generative AI gave us ideas, but we made them real—and now our community looks brighter than ever."

Grandma, watching proudly from the crowd, smiled. "Not bad for a couple of tech superheroes," she whispered.

Prompt Engineering Practice

Scenario

Tia and Jay want to help decorate their neighborhood block party, but they don't have art supplies. Their grandmother shows them how to use Generative AI to design decorations. To get the best results, they need a clear and detailed prompt. Let's help them!

What kind of decorations do they need? (Banners, posters, table signs, etc.)

Bad Prompt: *"Write me a song."*
Good Prompt: *"Write a happy, short song about a dog who loves to play in the park."*

Be very clear and detailed.

What theme or colors should the decorations have? (Summer, carnival, bright colors, etc.)

Write the final prompt!

Design decorations for a...

Work with an adult to test your prompt!

Nia's Robot Rescue Plan

UNIT 5

Unit 5 - Vocabulary Words

Read each vocabulary word and its definition. As you read the story, circle each vocabulary word when you find it.

1. **Recalibration:** Adjusting a machine to make it work better or more accurately.
2. **Blueprint:** A detailed plan or drawing that shows how to build something.
3. **Precision:** Doing something carefully and exactly, without mistakes.
4. **Ingenuity:** Using creativity and cleverness to solve a problem.

Nia's Robot Rescue Plan

Nia loved the hum of robots. As president of her school's Robotics Club, she spent hours building, coding, and dreaming up ways technology could make life easier.

This year, her club had their biggest idea yet: a robot designed to clean up the school's messy community garden. "We'll call it Eco-Bot," Nia said, sketching its features on the whiteboard. "It'll pick up trash, pull weeds, and even plant flowers!"

The team worked hard for weeks, assembling gears, writing code, and testing Eco-Bot in the garden. By the time the annual School Science Showcase approached, Eco-Bot was ready. Or so they thought.

The day before the event, disaster struck. When they tested Eco-Bot one last time, its gripper arm froze halfway through picking up a soda can, and its wheels spun making donuts in the dirt.

"What's wrong with it?" asked Malik, the club's top coder, frantically checking his laptop.

Nia frowned, crouching beside the robot. "I don't know, but if we don't fix it by tomorrow, we'll have nothing to show!"

Back in the robotics lab, Nia paced nervously as the team examined Eco-Bot. Malik rewrote lines of code while another teammate, Sofia, checked the wiring. Nothing worked.

"We need fresh ideas," Sofia said, frustrated.

Nia remembered something her science teacher had mentioned during class: Generative AI. "Wait!" she said, snapping her fingers. "There's a tool we can use—the Idea Machine!"

"What's that?" asked Malik, looking up from his laptop.

"It's a computer program called Generative AI. It can brainstorm ideas and suggest solutions when we're stuck," Nia explained. "We give it a problem, and it comes up with ideas to help us solve it. It's not perfect, but it might give us a starting point."

Nia opened her tablet and typed:
How do you fix a robot arm that won't move?
Within seconds, the AI responded:

- *Check for mechanical blockages.*
- *Update the motor's calibration.*
- *Use an alternative design for the arm.*

Sofia's eyes widened. "We haven't checked the motor's calibration yet!"

"And an alternative design could work if nothing else does," Malik added, looking hopeful.

The team divided up tasks based on the Idea Machine's suggestions.

"Malik, recalibrate the motor," Nia instructed. "Sofia, check the gripper arm for blockages. I'll use the AI to brainstorm a backup plan in case we need a new design."

Nia pasted the code that was responsible for the grippers function into the text box: **This controls a robot arm for picking up small objects in a garden. It is currently glitching. Scan the code for errors and then provide an alternative design.**

The Idea Machine returned the code that suggested a claw-like design using simple materials like rubber bands and PVC pipes. Nia sketched the idea, and the team started assembling it as a backup.

The recalibration worked—mostly. Eco-Bot's arm moved again, but it was slow and clunky. "It's better, but it's not enough," Malik admitted.

"Let's test the backup arm and the new code it provided," Nia said. The team swapped out the original arm for the new design and updated the code, following the Idea Machine's blueprint. It wasn't perfect, but the claw moved smoothly and could grip objects better than before.

Sofia ran Eco-Bot through a final test. It rolled across the garden, picking up trash and placing it in the recycling bin. When it finished planting a small flower, the team cheered.

The next day at the School Science Showcase, Eco-Bot stole the show. Parents and teachers gathered around to watch as it cleaned the garden with precision.

"This is incredible!" said Ms. Vega, the science teacher. "You turned a setback into an even better design."

After the event, Nia addressed the team. "The Idea Machine helped us get unstuck, but it was our teamwork and creativity that made this happen. We didn't give up, and that's what made Eco-Bot a success."

As they packed up, Malik grinned. "Who knew the Idea Machine could be such a good teammate?"

Nia laughed. "Maybe we should call it our Honorary Club Member."

The team walked away proud, knowing they had not only fixed their robot but also learned how to tackle problems with ingenuity and persistence.

Prompt Engineering Practice

Scenario

Nia and her Robotics Club built Eco-Bot, a robot that cleans the school's garden. But right before the Science Showcase, it stopped working! Nia needs to use Generative AI to help troubleshoot the problem. To get the best results, she needs a clear and detailed prompt. Let's help her!

What problem is Eco-Bot having? (Not moving, sensor issues, battery dead, etc.)

Bad Prompt: *"Plan a field trip."*
Good Prompt: *"Plan a field trip for 5th graders to a science museum with hands-on exhibits."*

e very clear and detailed.

What details can make this prompt more specific?

Write the final prompt!

Troubleshoot a robot that...

Work with an adult to test your prompt!

The Idea Machine

UNIT 6

Unit 6 - Vocabulary Words

Read each vocabulary word and its definition. As you read the story, circle each vocabulary word when you find it.

1. **Community Fundraiser:** An event where people come together to raise money for something important.
2. **Measure:** To find out the size or length of something, often to make sure it fits or works.

The Idea Machine

Every Friday, Maya and her friends rushed to their neighborhood library for the best part of the week: story time. Miss Rosa, the librarian, always had a new story ready, full of magical adventures, brave heroes, and talking animals.

But today, when Maya entered the library, something was wrong. Miss Rosa was frowning at a soggy pile of books.

"The storm last night caused the roof to leak," she explained. "All our storybooks are ruined. I'm so sorry, kids. I don't have anything to read today."

Maya's friend Jay gasped. "But storytime is our favorite! What are we going to do now?"

Maya looked around at the other kids' sad faces. Storytime wasn't just fun—it was important. "Maybe we can make our own stories," she said slowly.

Jay frowned. "How? We don't know how to write a bunch of stories, and it would take forever!"

Maya thought hard. Then she remembered something her grandmother had shown her recently. "What if we use the Idea Machine?" she suggested.

Back at her apartment, Alina gathered her friends around her family's laptop. She had been experimenting with a program her teacher had introduced in school: Generative AI.

"They call it the Idea Machine because you type in a problem, and it gives you ideas to help you solve them," Alina explained.

"Like a robot that can think and solves all problems?" David asked skeptically.

"Not exactly," Alina said. "It doesn't think like we do — it uses patterns it learned to give suggestions for possible paths forward. But we're the ones who decide what works."

"Let's try it," Max said, bouncing on his toes.

Alina typed into the search bar: **How can we fix a playground without money?** The screen blinked, then displayed a list of ideas:

- Reuse old materials, like tires and wood.
- Ask neighbors for tools and supplies.
- Host a community fundraiser to raise money for repairs.

"These are awesome!" Jamila said, pointing at the screen.

"My mom has old tires in the backyard," David offered.

"And I bet my uncle has rope," Jamila added.

Alina smiled. "Let's brainstorm a plan using all these ideas."

The kids sat on the floor with notebooks and pencils. "Step one: gather materials," Alina said, jotting it down.

"Jamila and David can ask their families for tires, rope, and anything else we might use," Max suggested.

"Step two: design posters for a fundraiser," Jamila added.

Alina nodded. "The Idea Machine can help with that too!" She typed: Design a poster for a playground fundraiser. The AI created colorful designs with slogans like "**Bring Back the Fun!**" and "**Swing into Action!**"

"Perfect," Max said, copying the designs onto paper with crayons.

The next day, the kids gathered their materials. David's uncle donated sturdy rope, Jamila's mom found two old tires, and the AI helped them brainstorm a safe way to patch the slide.

But their first attempt didn't go well. When they tied the tire swing to the frame, it hung too low, and when Jamila sat on it, her feet dragged on the ground.

"Oops," David said, scratching his head.

"It's okay," Alina said. "Let's measure the rope better and try again."

At the fundraiser, things were slow at first. Only a few neighbors stopped by, and Max looked worried. "What if nobody comes?"

"We just need to spread the word," Alina said. She walked from booth to booth, talking to families and inviting them to join.

Slowly, more people arrived, and soon the park was filled with kids, parents, and grandparents.

By the end of the day, they had enough donations to buy paint and tools to finish the repairs.

The following week, the playground was transformed. The kids painted the slide bright blue, hung two sturdy tire swings, and even fixed the merry-go-round. On Saturday, they hosted a "Playground Celebration Day," and the whole neighborhood came to play.

"This looks amazing!" Jamila said, swinging back and forth.

"We didn't just fix the playground," David said. "We made it better."

"And we didn't do it alone," Alina added. "The Idea Machine gave us ideas, but we made them real."

Grandma, watching proudly, called out, "Tech superheroes, that's what you are!"

Max grinned. "I like the sound of that."

As the sun set and laughter filled the air, the kids knew they had done something special. They had taken a broken playground and turned it into a place where their community could come together again.

Prompt Engineering Practice

Scenario

Maya and her friends love storytime at the library, but a storm ruined all the books! They decide to create their own stories using Generative AI. To get the best results, they need a clear and detailed prompt. Let's help them!

What type of story do they want to create?
(Adventure, mystery, fantasy, etc.)

Bad Prompt: *"Make a toy."*
Good Prompt: *"Design a stuffed animal that looks like a baby dragon and changes colors."*

Be very clear and detailed.

Who are the main characters, and what makes them unique? What is the main problem or challenge in the story?

Write the final prompt!

Write a story about...

Work with an adult to test your prompt!

Milo's Music Mission

UNIT 7

Unit 7 - Vocabulary Words

Read each vocabulary word and its definition. As you read the story, circle each vocabulary word when you find it.

1. Melody: A sequence of musical notes that make up the main tune of a song.
2. Riff: A short, catchy musical phrase often repeated in a song.
3. Transition: A way to connect different parts of a song smoothly.
4. Improvise: To make up something on the spot, like a musical tune or rhythm.

Milo's Music Mission

Milo tapped his drumsticks nervously against his knee as the other band members argued. Their school band had been invited to perform at the annual community festival—a huge honor—but they hadn't come up with a song yet.

"I think we should play something jazzy," suggested Elena, the saxophonist.

"But I want something upbeat, like a rock anthem!" said Jonah, who played the electric guitar.

"I just want us to agree," Milo mumbled, looking at his drums.
The festival was only two weeks away, and they were stuck. No one could agree on a song, and none of their ideas felt exciting enough for the big stage.

"What if we create our own song?" Milo suggested.

"Create our own? That sounds impossible," Elena said.

"It's not impossible," Milo replied. "We just need a little help."

Milo's older sister, Zoe, overheard their conversation while tuning her violin. "Why don't you use a music generator?" she suggested.

"A what?" Jonah asked, raising an eyebrow.

"It's a tool that uses Generative AI to create new music," Zoe explained. "You tell it what style you want—like jazz or rock—

and it gives you a melody to start with. Then you can add your own touches to make it yours!"

Milo's eyes lit up. "That sounds perfect! Can you show us how it works?"

Zoe pulled up a music-generating website on her tablet. "Just type in what you want, like 'upbeat jazz with a catchy rhythm.' It'll create a short melody you can listen to."

Jonah typed: **rock music with a powerful guitar solo. The AI played a simple melody.**

"This is awesome!" he said, strumming along on his guitar. Elena added her own prompt: **smooth jazz with a groovy saxophone.** The AI created another melody, and Elena started playing it, swaying with the rhythm.

"This is actually fun," she admitted.

Inspired, the band decided to create their song by blending everyone's ideas.

"We'll make a mash-up," Milo said. "Let's take the best parts of each melody the AI gave us and build from there."

They worked together, combining the guitar riff from Jonah's melody, the saxophone tune from Elena's, and a catchy drumbeat Milo improvised.

As they played, Milo typed new prompts into the AI to add finishing touches:

- Background melody for a piano.
- A dramatic intro for the drums.

The AI gave them ideas that made their song even more exciting.

The band practiced their new song every day, but it wasn't perfect at first.

"The transition between the jazz part and the rock part feels awkward," Elena pointed out.

"Let's smooth it out by adding a drum solo," Milo suggested. He typed a new prompt: Create a short drum solo to connect these two melodies.

The AI provided a rhythm, and Milo adjusted it to fit their song. After a few tries, it worked perfectly.

On the day of the festival, they performed their song for the first time. The crowd clapped along to the beat, cheering when Jonah's guitar solo hit and swaying during Elena's saxophone melody.

After the performance, the mayor approached the band. "That was incredible! How did you come up with such a unique sound?"

Milo smiled. "We used technology to get started, but it was teamwork that made it special."

Jonah nodded. "The music generator gave us ideas, but the creativity came from us."

As they packed up their instruments, Elena added, "Maybe next, we'll create an entire album!"

Prompt Engineering Practice

Scenario

Milo's band needs a new song for their school festival, but they can't agree on what to play. Milo's sister introduces them to a music generator powered by Generative AI. To get the best results, they need a clear and detailed prompt. Let's help them!

What style of music do they want? (Rock, pop, jazz, hip-hop, etc.)

Bad Prompt: *"Make a video game character."*
Good Prompt: *"Create a futuristic hero with glowing armor and the ability to control time."*

Be very clear and detailed.

What should the song be about? (School spirit, friendship, chasing dreams, etc.)

Write the final prompt!

Create a song about...

Work with an adult to test your prompt!

The Code of Curiosity

UNIT 8

Unit 8 - Vocabulary Words

Read each vocabulary word and its definition. As you read the story, circle each vocabulary word when you find it.

1. **Leaderboard:** A chart that shows who's doing the best in a game or activity.
2. **Recycle:** To turn old things into something new instead of throwing them away.
3. **Innovation:** A new idea or way of doing something to solve a problem.
4. **Laminated:** Covered in a plastic layer to protect something, like a poster or card.

The Code of Curiosity

Aria, Kian, and Samira sat on the steps of the Meadowridge Library after school, surrounded by notebooks and empty juice boxes.

"We need a great idea," Kian said, tapping his pencil on his forehead. "Something to fix a problem in town."

"But what problem?" Samira asked, doodling in her notebook.
Aria thought for a moment. "What about all the trash in the park?

Every time I play soccer there, I see bottles and wrappers everywhere."

Samira nodded. "It's the same at the river. People just leave garbage everywhere. It's gross!"

"But what can we do about it?" Kian asked. "We're just kids. We don't have tools or money to clean up the whole town."

Just then, Mrs. Patel, the librarian, stepped outside. "You kids look stuck," she said with a kind smile.

"We are," Aria admitted. "We need an idea for the Innovation Challenge, but we don't have anything good yet."

Mrs. Patel tilted her head. "Have you heard of Generative AI?"

Inside the library, Mrs. Patel led them to a small computer station. "Generative AI is a type of computer program that helps people come up with ideas and solutions. You tell it what you need, and it makes suggestions based on your input."

She opened the Idea Machine and typed: **How can we reduce litter in a small town with simple resources?**

In seconds, the screen displayed ideas:

- *Create a "litter leaderboard" to track who picks up the most trash.*
- *Start an art contest using recycled materials.*
- *Place fun, decorated trash cans around the park to encourage people to use them.*

"Whoa!" Kian said, leaning closer. "It's like it's brainstorming with us!"

Mrs. Patel nodded. "It's not magic—it's a tool. It gives you ideas, but it's up to you to make them work."

Inspired, the three friends sat at the library table, sketching and writing.

"What if we combine two of the ideas?" Samira suggested. "We could make a trash-picking game and reward people with prizes made from recycled stuff."

"That's genius!" Kian said. "We could call it 'Meadowridge Clean Team.'"

"And we can ask local shops to donate small prizes, like snacks or books," Aria added.

Using the Idea Machine, they brainstormed catchy slogans like "Clean Up, Level Up!" and "Turn Trash Into Treasure!" They also asked the AI for help designing a colorful poster to explain the rules of their game.

The next day, they took their idea to the park to test it out. They created a simple leaderboard on a poster and invited kids and families to join the cleanup game.

Some people were excited, but others were skeptical.
"Why should I bother?" asked Mr. Harris, the local shopkeeper. "The park will just get messy again."

Aria explained, "That's why it's a game! If everyone helps, we can keep it clean for good. And we'll have prizes to make it fun."

They also ran into problems with their homemade posters—they smudged when it rained. Using the AI again, they came up with ideas for sturdier designs and even used the library's printer to make laminated flyers.

By the end of the week, more people had joined the game, including Mr. Harris, who offered free ice cream to anyone who collected the most trash in a day.

On the day of the Community Innovation Challenge, Aria, Kian, and Samira presented their project. They showed photos of clean parks and happy neighbors and explained how the Idea Machine helped them come up with a plan.

When the judges announced the winners, the Meadowridge Clean Team took first place! The judges praised their creativity and how their project brought the community together.

As they held their recycled trophy, Kian grinned. "I guess we're pretty good at this innovation stuff after all."

"And now the park looks amazing," Samira added.

"Yeah," Aria said. "It's not just about the trophy. We actually made a difference."

Prompt Engineering Practice

Scenario

Aria, Kian, and Samira want to solve a problem in their town for the Community Innovation Challenge. They decide to use Generative AI to come up with creative ideas. To get the best results, they need a clear and detailed prompt. Let's help them!

Identify what you want to draw.

What problem in their town do they want to solve?
(Pollution, traffic, lack of playgrounds, etc.)

Bad Prompt: *"Make an ice cream flavor."*
Good Prompt: *"Create a new ice cream flavor inspired by tropical fruits with a crunchy topping."*

Be very clear and detailed.

What kind of solution are they looking for? (A new invention, a community program, a better way to do something?)

Write the final prompt!

Come up with an idea for...

Work with an adult to test your prompt!

"Let us remember: One book, one pen, one child and one teacher can change the world."

- Malala Yousafzai

Remember, the world is full of opportunities.

More Young & Brilliant Books

For more Young & Brilliant books and resources, scan the QR Code below or visit us at www.youngandbrilliant.org

www.ingramcontent.com/pod-product-compliance
Lightning Source LLC
LaVergne TN
LVHW070855210926
848482LV00016B/944